What's in the cupboards and

What's

in the drawer? The bread on
the counter, the crumbs on
the floor, the smells of

Cooking

the sound of stirring, and the
pleasant hum of mixers purring.
Enter, sniff, and feel the thrill.
The kitchen is a wonderland,
wander in and understand.

To Auggie and Achilles, no matter where
you are or where I am, I will always love you.
JDS

For Ms. Dusty and my favorite
2nd grade readers at P.S. 32
JR

Phaidon Press Inc.
65 Bleecker Street
New York, NY 10012

phaidon.com

First published 2017
© 2017 Phaidon Press Limited
Text copyright © Joshua David Stein
Illustrations copyright © Julia Rothman

Artwork illustrated using ink and gouache.

ISBN 978 0 7148 7508 8 (US edition)
001-0817

Designed by Meagan Bennett

Printed in China

What's Cooking?

by Joshua David Stein

illustrated by Julia Rothman

a strip of potato,

and a slice of tomato,

can I fry a
scoop of gelato?

Actually, yes!

Gelato is a type of ice cream, and fried ice cream is a real dessert.

It's warm on the outside, cold on the inside, and delicious all around.

Can

I

can

clams?

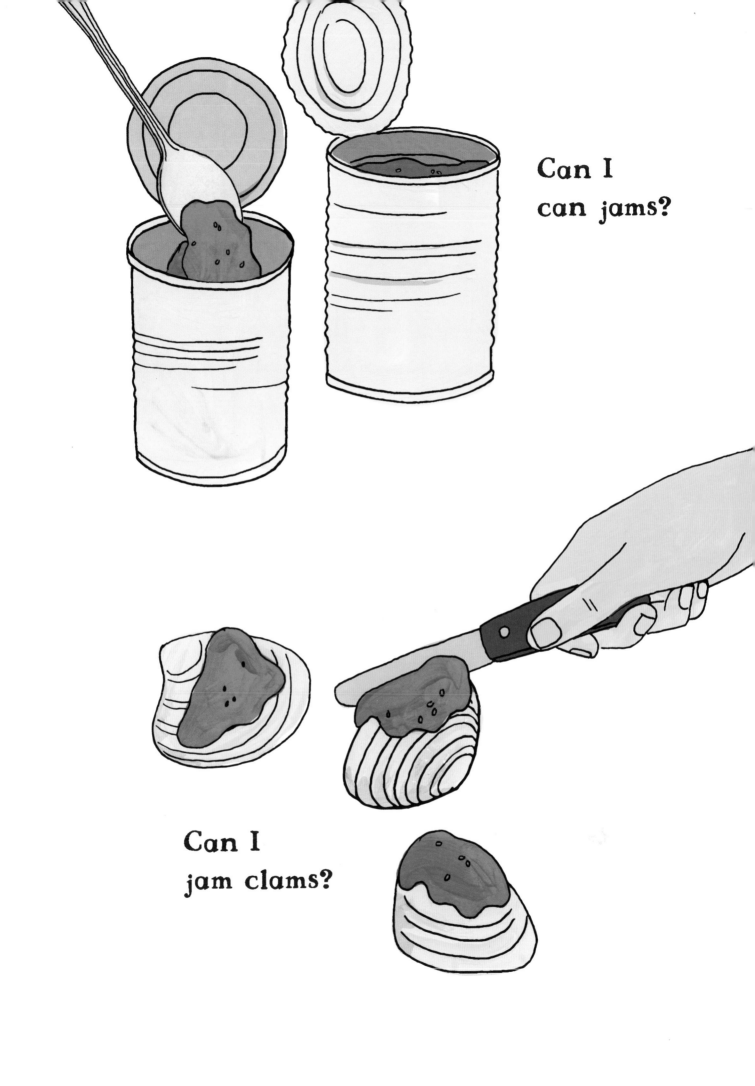

Can I
can jams?

Can I
jam clams?

Clams you can can, chopped up in clam juice.

Jam you can can, and you can jar it too.

And you can't jam clams, but
you can certainly jelly them.
That's called clams en gelée
(which is a fancy word for jelly).

Squeeze a grape ...   juice.

Freeze the juice ...   Popsicle.

Squeeze a Popsicle ...

puddle!

If I toss a salad,
can I throw a salad?

A salad can be
tossed to mix up
all the ingredients.

But it should *never*
be thrown.

Dough you can throw, though.

That's how pizza is made.
It is thrown up in the
air and spun around
and around.

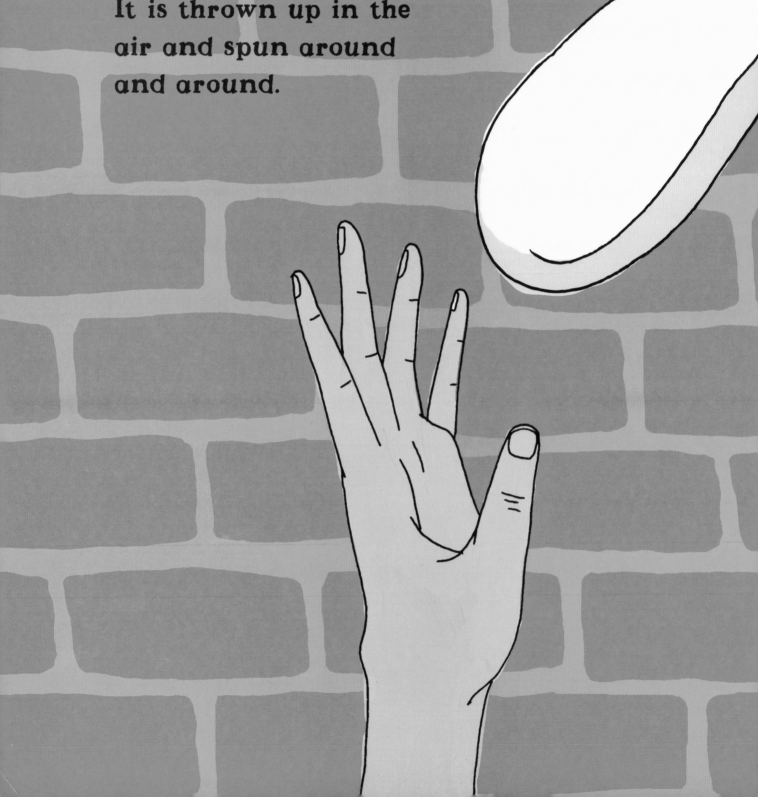

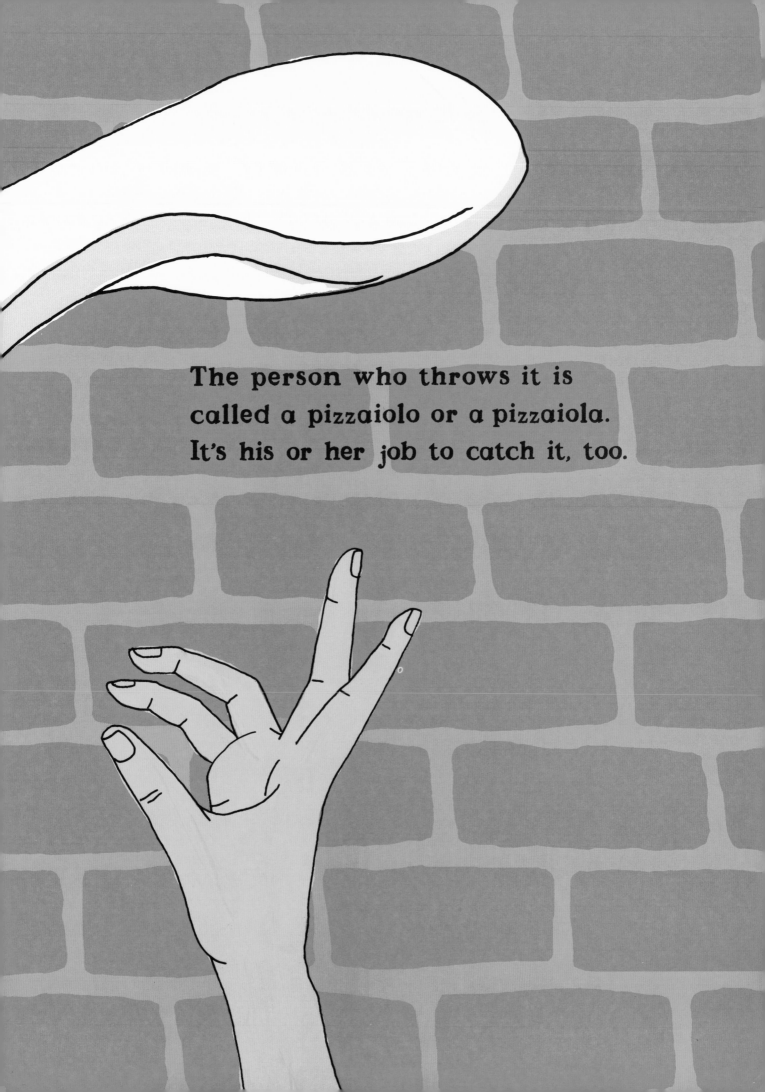

The person who throws it is
called a pizzaiolo or a pizzaiola.
It's his or her job to catch it, too.

E G

Beaten

Broken

Scrambled

Fried

G S

Cured
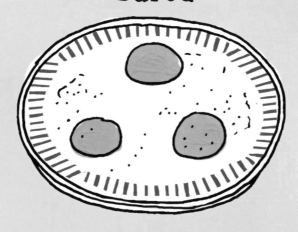

Coddled

Baked

and Tried

If turkeys are stuffed
with stuffing, what
else can I stuff?

Lots of stuff.

You can stuff
peppers with rice,

and cabbage
with meat,

and even meat with
meat. That's called
a ballotine.

Well, if I stuff stuffing,
can I dump dumplings?

No, but you can stuff dumplings...

with pork for
gyoza in Japan,

with cheese for
pierogi in Ukraine,

with soup for
xiaolongbao
(soup dumplings)
in China!

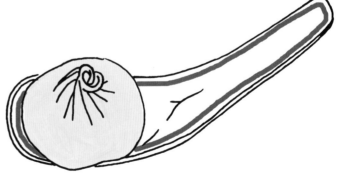

Is this a
very old grape
or a
very new raisin?

If I eat left overs, can
I eat left unders?

It depends—left
under where?

Do frozen peas grow
on frozen trees?

No. Frozen peas start off as fresh peas, grown on vines.

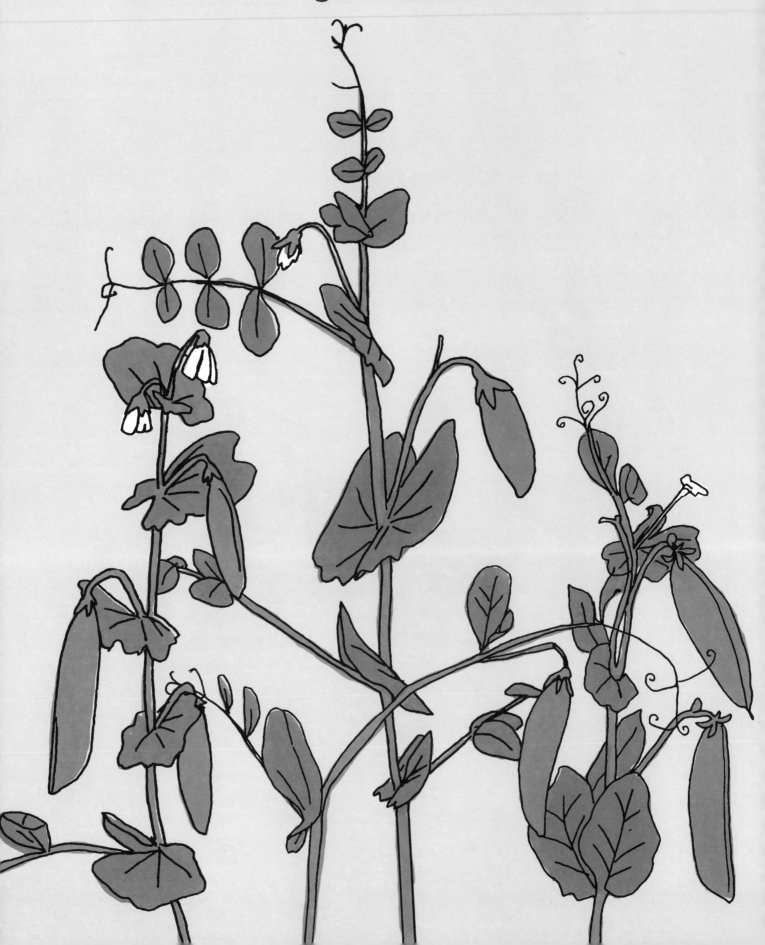

But after they're harvested, they're
frozen so they last longer.

The spinach is creamed and the snow peas are steamed. The garlic is minced and the lettuce is rinsed. The cucumbers are cubed and the squash has been squared. The tomatoes are stewed and the parsnip is pared.

The beef has been roasted. The bread has been toasted. All the eggs have been boiled. The salmon is broiled. Melon is scooped. Lemon is zested. Cookies are cooked. Cookies are tested.

Now the only question is...

...who does
the dishes?

Oh, a potato! Can I...

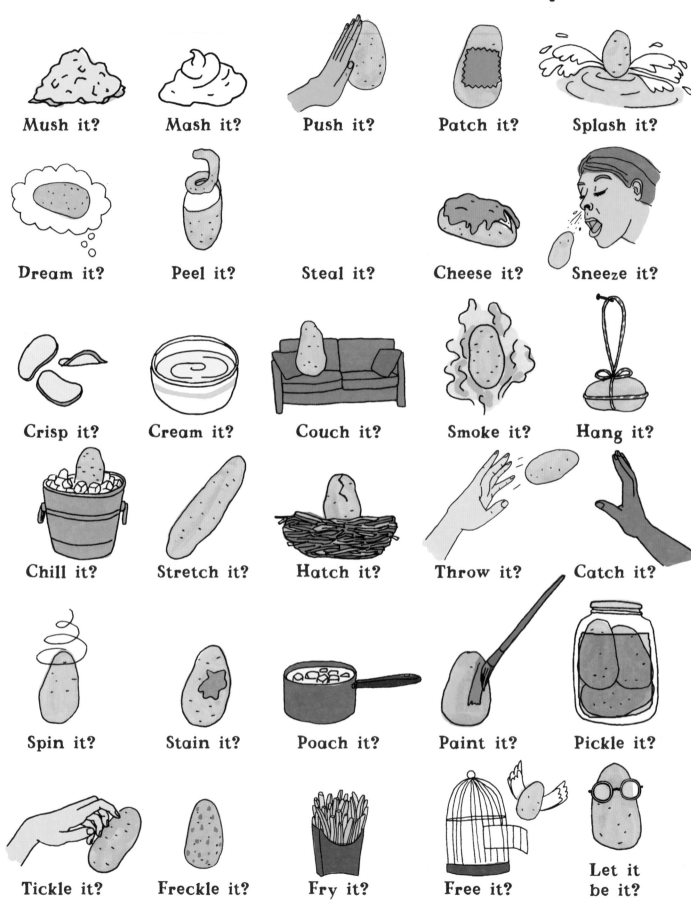

Mush it? Mash it? Push it? Patch it? Splash it?

Dream it? Peel it? Steal it? Cheese it? Sneeze it?

Crisp it? Cream it? Couch it? Smoke it? Hang it?

Chill it? Stretch it? Hatch it? Throw it? Catch it?

Spin it? Stain it? Poach it? Paint it? Pickle it?

Tickle it? Freckle it? Fry it? Free it? Let it be it?